A BROWN GIRL'S BOOK OF ETIQUETTE

"Tips of Refinement, Leveling Up and Doing it with Class"

KAREMA MCGHEE

©COPYRIGHT 2021

All rights reserved. No part of this publication may be reproduced, stored in retrieval system, or transmitted, in any form or by any means, electronic, mechanical, photocopying, recording, or otherwise, without prior permission from the publisher.

LUXINOUS PUBLISHING COMPANY

P.O. BOX 732

MEBANE, NC 27302.

ISBN: 978-1-7-353636-6-0

TABLE OF CONTENTS

DEDICATION -- 1

ACKNOWLEDGEMENTS ---------------------------------- 2

INTRODUCTION -- 3

WEARING PERFUME --- 8

ANNOUNCEMENT ETIQUTTE --------------------------- 13

FINE DINING ETIQUETTE ---------------------------------- 19

ENTERTAINING AT HOME/DINNERS/HOSTING GUESTS -- 25

ALL ABOUT WINES --- 32

WINE ATTRIBUTES --- 37

ARE YOU APPROACHABLE? ----------------------------- 40

Dedication

This work is dedicated to my mother who forbade me from sitting on her front porch with boys. Although I never did it, she made it noticeably clear that I was to never do it. She was very conscious of how things are often perceived.

Momma, we did it.

Acknowledgements

I want to acknowledge my early Muslim upbringing; I am in debt. Most of my adult personality is deeply rooted in all things from birth up until about age eleven. These moments were most religious for my family, and much of who I am today is deeply rooted in the behaviors taught during those early years.

I acknowledge that Islam had a profound effect on my developing mind and in building my personality. It was responsible for getting me through doors that would have otherwise been closed to others.

With an extreme emphasis on manners, mannerism, kindness, honesty, and compassion for others, I know this discipline is what leads to this book.

Introduction

Growing up in the late '70s was a very fragile time for little brown girls in hoods across America. Fragile in the sense that the early '70s had witnessed a revolution take place in Black America. The "I'm Black and I'm Proud" movement had started in 1968 with James Brown screaming it from stage tops in brown pants and crop tops.

The late '70s were riding the wave of years earlier of Huey P. Newton, Bobby Seale, and Elbert Howard from the Black Panthers. Creating self-sufficient neighborhoods and schools, creating free lunch programs for its inner-city youth, and protecting its neighborhoods from police brutality was the pride of Black America during this time.

Black women sported their natural hair and rocked their red, black, and green flags with pride, and it was still looming in the late '70s. The civil rights movement had seen its heights as Martin Luther

King and Malcolm X had become legends by this time, and the Nation of Islam (NOI) made its way to Black men across America. I was born in this era.

The seemly progress and regression of Black Nationalism was bound to come to a screeching halt in the early '80s with the crack epidemic. The crack epidemic plagued Black neighborhoods, disrupted, and dismantled families. The wealth gap that was closing with the Black Pride Movement had been stopped.

Black women carried the weight of Black America at this time as they were forced to live with the addiction plagued households that later resulted in fatherless households due to new legislation and strict laws on drugs that specifically targeted the same neighborhoods impacted by the crack epidemic. Those times were fragile because Black men were disproportionately being incarcerated as the drugs flooded the neighborhoods.

In true Black woman form, she took the hits, grabbed hold of what was left, got tougher, fought harder, and got stronger. What the world now views as the strong Black woman, or what some characterize as the angry Black woman, we are really looking at a race of women who grew up during a time that was fragile but required her to be hard—hard enough so she could survive. We are looking at the remnants and the impact of a generation of women plagued by historic happenings, environmental conditioning, and social overcoming.

This book is my way of alerting Brown girls across America and beyond that we can relax a bit. We are not in this fight alone. The days of carrying the entire weight of the family on our backs are over. We have arrived, and the world is listening. Our voices are louder now more than ever before.

As we are climbing the social ladder, making our way in corporate America, finding our way into politics, building million-dollar businesses, it is our duty to reclaim our feminine charm by way of embracing etiquette ideas for smoother social interactions.

Although the social injustices of yesterday are still prevalent today, we are not the same people we were yesterday. We have made a tremendous leap forward despite pushing through the crack epidemic and the AIDS epidemic and the many other obstacles Black people faced here in the Americas and around the world. It is in our best interest to keep pushing forward despite the circumstances.

To further evolve as women and to embrace new ways of being that are in line with our future and not so much our past, I wrote this book for the Brown girls who wrestle with controlling the emotions shown on their faces when they are displeased or the Brown girls who know no other way to be real except to tell you the truth no matter how hurtful it is, especially those Brown girls who, for whatever reason, people seem to think they are angry all the time even when they are not speaking. I am writing this book for all the Brown girls who believe that there is always room for improvement, but they do not know where to start.

This book is for the seeker, any woman looking to lean into a bit of etiquette and developing her feminine charm because the truth is most of our mothers did not come from times of finishing schools nor did they have time to train. They were far too busy trying to survive.

The objective of this book is to expose you to new ways of being, new ways of doing, and new ways of thinking, all in a way that can possibly improve social interactions, improve important relationships, develop character, improve your feminine charm, and give you tips on the basic things, like how to invite guests over formally or informally for a dinner, how to compose a work email, how to set a dinner table, and how to avoid common etiquette mistakes.

The things we will go over in this book are things I have learned the hard way or from my mother and my own experiences. I am hoping the things I share with you in this book will improve your life as much as they have mine.

Wearing Perfume

Every woman should have a signature scent, one that is uniquely hers. However, when it comes to the etiquette of wearing fragrances, there are few things to keep in mind.

Things to remember about fragrance etiquette:

1. TIME AND PLACE

Your work fragrance is most certainly not the same fragrance you would wear on date night. Although you might enjoy the smell of your favorite date night fragrance, it may be inappropriate for work. Your work fragrance should be light and gentle with a low sillage, which means the fragrance sticks closer to your body and is less likely to fill a whole room and leave a trail when you walk. I completely understand women who want to be unforgettable but consider your environment. When it comes to etiquette, we are most certainly considering others in our actions.

A light fragrance is most appropriate during work hours because it is less likely to become a nuisance to others or spark allergies in coworkers while a high sillage and heavier scent is most appropriate for night.

An example of a low sillage daytime fragrance is Dolce & Gabbana Light Blue. It is worn by many and is extremely popular. A not-so-known suggestion would be Pasha De Cartier instead, an ole time favorite, or Creed's Love in White. Although these suggestions have a light sillage, the longevity of the fragrances are not compromised.

If you must live on the edge a bit and are looking for a fragrance that will get you many compliments without causing a nuisance in the office, Eau De Magnolia by Frederic Malle is the perfect floral fragrance for the ultimate feminine experience while at work. An example of a high sillage unforgettable nighttime/date night fragrance is Boadicea the Victorious Blue Sapphire and Baccarat Rouge 540 by Maison Francis Kurkdjian. These fragrances are unforgettable.

2. AVOID SPRAYING FRAGRANCE ON YOUR CLOTHES

A common practice for people looking to prolong their fragrances is to spray the fragrance on their clothes. From an etiquette perspective, if you are in a social gathering or a networking event and embrace some unknowing person only for them to be stuck with your fragrance on their fine threads, you stand a chance of creating a bad impression, or perhaps you'll always be known as the person who left a terrible scent on an unsuspecting person $i dollar shirt.

In etiquette, remember, to be socially correct, we must consider everyone we engage with. However, if you fear your fragrance will fade throughout the day, perhaps its time to explore a finer scent. In the fragrance world, there is an etiquette to applying fine fragrances and good reasons behind the ideas.

The idea of dabbing a small amount behind the ears, on your wrist, or behind your knees or lower neck is because those areas of the body are either pulse points or are areas that warm up quickly with movement, causing the perfume to react with your body heat or body chemistry and emit a fragrance. It is science. Fabrics do not create a unique scent specific to the person, so to get the best out of your fragrances, apply them to your body and let science take care of the rest.

3. NEVER SPRAY AND GO

Have you ever sprayed your fragrance in the work bathroom after freshening up only for some strange person to come in complaining, "Oh, my gosh, who is wearing all of that perfume?" If this has ever happened to you, please note that this is quite common. Perfume spray from the bottle is often off putting, especially at first sniff. If you must freshen up throughout the day, try using a perfume solid.

It is much more decreet, much more personable, and easier to carry. Many perfumes come in perfume solids, but for some reason, people are only aware of perfume sprays. The next time you visit your favorite perfume counter, ask them to show you the same fragrance in a solid.

My suggestion would be to spray your fragrance on in the morning and apply your solid throughout the day if you need to. However, please keep in mind that just because it is a solid does not mean it is not as strong. In fact, the perfume solid is normally much more concentrated, but it will save you from the embarrassment of freshly sprayed perfume. Always keep a solid in your purse just in case you need to reapply.

Announcement Etiqutte

The most important moments of our lives are to be shared with those we love and respect. Sharing those moments makes them that much more enjoyable. Special moments become unforgettable when we invite others to share in our joy, but even inviting others in, etiquette should be followed out of respect for those we love.

1. BABY ARRIVALS AND SHOWER ANNOUNCEMENT

One of life's most celebrated times is the arrival of a new baby. The excitement is almost uncontainable.

When it comes to announcing a pregnancy or the arrival of a newborn, it is most important to allow the parents' privacy and allow them time to make the announcement as they see fit.

You would not want to be that one person who let the cat out of the bag about someone's pregnancy or about the arrival of a child without consulting the parents. If the announcement is not your own, be sure to reserve your excitement and allow the parents to share their special moments with whomever they see fit.

Baby showers, gender reveals, possible due dates, whereabouts, and so forth are just as sensitive. When you protect the private information of others, you show them how much you value them. It also shows how mature and thoughtful you are, which, in turn, builds trust. People love being around people they can trust. You will most likely be on the invited list if you can add being the gatekeeper of others' private moments to your personality. It is a classy way to be.

If you are organizing a baby shower or gender reveal on behalf of an expecting mother, here are three tips to keep in mind.

a) Arrange the shower no later than six weeks before the due date.
b) Be sure to discuss the guest list with both parents if possible.
c) Send out the invitations no later than four weeks before the event.

For sure, there are many things you will want to consider, like venue location, cost, transportation of the expecting mother, food services, and decorations, but you most certainly want to remember that this event is on behalf of the expecting parents and sharing this moment with those they love. The event is not about you. Remember to leave yourself out of the equation, and they will forever be thankful.

2. GRADUATION ANNOUNCEMENT

Graduations can be an extremely emotional event in a person's life because they mark a milestone reached by the graduate. In the case of high school graduations, generally most schools give out a limited number of tickets, which are directly connected to how many people each student can invite. If you are the parent of a soon-to-be graduate, it is important to identify the number of tickets allowed per student eight weeks before the graduation date. This gives you and your graduate enough time to decide who should be invited to the event, gives you time to send out the invites, and receive the RSVPs back. When you send out your invitations, be sure to get them out soon enough, so if you have family or friends who live out of town and need to make travel arrangements, they will have enough time to do so without worry.

3. WEDDING ANNOUNCEMENT

My first marriage's announcement was first in our local newspapers before my invitations went out. The announcement had been published as the entire city was invited to our park wedding. I made many mistakes from an etiquette perspective but learned much in this process.

I will attempt to save you from the embarrassment I felt as things did not always go as planned. The first thing I want you to know is that you are going to run into many issues just in the announcement and invitation phase of the marriage alone. Here are my top five lessons. Perhaps they will save you time and money.

a) Remember that the announcement of the engagement and the actual wedding announcement are two separate announcements. Wedding announcements are generally sent the day after the wedding. It is normally sent to loved ones who could not attend the wedding, friends you could not invite, family members who live abroad, and colleagues and other business associates.

b) If you are using your local newspaper for your engagement announcement, be sure that you get a copy of the ad before it runs to press. A misspelled name in print can ruin an entire announcement.

c) Be sure to proofread your announcements even if they are being done by a professional. Take your time and read line by line to ensure that everything is correct. It's also not a bad idea to have your spouse read them as well. The more eyes before sending, the better. From an etiquette perspective anything within thirty days after the marriage is appropriate for wedding announcements.

d) If you are hiring a photographer to take engagement pictures and are using these as your actual announcement photos, be sure that you give the photographer at least five days to get the photos back to you. You might also want to get this agreement in writing. Many people stress when the photographer is delayed in getting photos back to them on time, but if you plan this out and communicate your expectations up front, it can lead to a smoother transaction.

If you have received a wedding announcement from a friend or loved one, it is generally accepted to share the news at this point as most announcements are sent to announce the union.

Fine Dining Etiquette

I had my first diner at a five-star restaurant, and I quickly learned I had not reached a level I thought I had. During dinner, I ordered a glass of Champagne. I learned quickly that was a bad move that exposed me as someone who had never experienced fine dining before.

This pivotal moment in my adult life really exposed me to a new level of social norms that I was for sure not accustomed to. My date at the time gently reached under the table, grabbed my hand, and said, "Beautiful, Champagne is better ordered before dinner to celebrate an important moment or at desert unless, of course, you are home. You can drink it as you wish." Would you like it for dessert? Instead of being offended or questing his gentle nudge, I responded, "Yes, desert is perfect." I have had a few more hiccups at high society dinners and corporate luncheons, and luckily for me, I have always been surrounded by people who were not afraid to give me a gentle nudge.

Here are some fine dining etiquette tips that can save you from embarrassment or moments of ignorance.

1. ORDERING CHAMPAGNE

a) Never order a bottle of Champagne when at a dinner party or a private dinner without the consent of everyone at the table. You can get their consent by asking the entire table, "How about a round of Champagne to celebrate?" Read the room to be sure everyone is in on it.

b) Champagne is generally a celebratory drink and should be ordered by the bottle when there are six people at the table. A full bottle for six splits perfectly. In the event there are more people at the table, be sure to order enough bottles so everyone can participate.

c) Never order less Champagne because you cannot afford multiple bottles to accommodate all who are present at the table. If you are unsure about your ability to accommodate, it is best to pass on ordering any at all. The last thing you want is three people at the table without a glass to lift in celebration because you could not accommodate them.
d) If you are ordering Champagne by the glass, be sure to remember that a glass of wine is much more rewarding. However, if you are dead set on having a glass for dessert, be sure to ask that your glass be poured from a new bottle.

I have been a wearer of red lipstick for over ten years. I especially wear it on date nights, and it's my signature makeup look for going out. This next lesson will help you with some tips on acceptable behaviors while dining.

My embarrassing moment happened as I was socially drinking a glass of red wine, chatting, and enjoying the evening, not realizing that around the rim of my glass was a trail of red puckered lipstick stains. Clearly, I had been enjoying not just the night but also my glass of red wine. It was brought to my attention in the most loving way. "Karema, ask for another glass of wine. Ask them to take the one you have."

I was so confused, so I responded, "Oh, no, this one is fine. I am almost done." She reached over and whispered, "Your glass is full of lipstick stains." I looked down and was appalled.

How could I not notice? Why was this not a natural thing for me to notice? I had hoped that she was the only one to notice, so I asked the waiter to collect my glass. It was at that moment that I scanned the table and noticed that my glass was the only glass trailed with lipstick stains. Here are a few tips to keep in mind while drinking and dining.

2. SIPPING FROM YOUR GLASS

a) If you are wearing a colored lipstick, be sure to sip from the same place on your glass each time you lift. The look of your glass after you engage is just as important as to how you hold you glass while sipping.
b) Be aware of your glass, take your time with each sip, and be mindful of the residue left

behind. A nasty glass can be a turn off for others at the table.
c) If you are attending a high society dinner or event, its best to wear a neutral lipstick. This will give you less to think about when engaging and allow you to enjoy your dinner without calculating how to sip from your glass. Even still, be mindful.
d) Never take sweeping gulps, especially when wine is involved. Sip slowly, allow the wine to find the taste buds in your mouth, and slowly lower your glass after you have fully tasted your sip. Allow moments of rest before picking up your glass again.
e) While enjoying wine, or any drink for that matter, with a stem, be sure to hold the glass closest to the base of the glass. Cupping a glass is common, but to be in line with fine dining ideas, hold your glass closest to the base/bottom of the stem.

3. QUICK TIPS

a) Never make an announcement to the table that you must go to the restroom or that you need to make or take a phone call. Just excuse yourself and take care of your business.

b) Using electronics at a table is poor behavior. Being fully engaged while dining is most appropriate and shows your true interest.
c) When placing your order, do not be in haste. Be sure that everyone at the table is ready and get a consensus before moving forward.
d) If you are attending a corporate event or a private dinner or having dinner at a luxury restaurant, be sure to be aware of your noise level. If you have ever been to a fine dining restaurant, you will notice that there is less talking and quieter music, and the noise volume is low. Loud talking and laughing can be a nuisance to others trying their best to enjoy their meal.
e) When you have finished your meal, remember your napkin is not to leave your lap and be placed on your plate. The only time your napkin leaves your lap is when you are patting debris from your mouth or when you are ready to leave. At this time, it is most appropriate for your napkin to be placed on your plate.
f.) Never reach across the table for anything. If there is something you need on the other side of the table, ask the person closest to the item to hand it to you.

Entertaining at Home/Dinners/Hosting Guests

Nothing else gives me more pleasure than hosting guests—both business and otherwise. As you move up the corporate ladder or as you make your way into wealthier and healthier circles, you find that it is a superpower being labeled a great hostess.

If you are hosting your husband's family from out of town, a dinner party, or a girls' night out at your home, there are some universal things you must know to create great experiences. The first thing you must remember is it is your goal and responsibility as the hostess to create a great experience for those in your space. Great hosts think about ways to improve someone's experience.

When it comes to etiquette in these instances, it boils down to selflessness and manners. That is all etiquette really is.

It stickily is manners and consideration for others. To give you an example of selflessness, let us assume your husband has family visiting from out of town. You have known it for weeks. The universal idea is that you are prepared for their visit.

However, at the last minute, you realize that the bed you had reserved for both the husband and wife is not big enough for them to be comfortable together, but it is too late to explore another option.

WHAT DO YOU DO? WHAT IS THE BEST OPTION?

a) Allow one to sleep on an air mattress while the other is in the bed in a neighboring room.
b) Offer a place for one to sleep on your couch.
c) Offer blankets for them both to sleep on the floor.

d) Offer an option for putting them up at a local hotel.
e) Offer your own bed.

First, let us consider the fact that this couple is married. Married people are most comfortable sleeping together while traveling, especially when traveling to new, different, or strange places. They also prefer to sleep near each other.

Placing one in one room and the other in another sounds okay if they have some place to lay their heads, but a great host considers a guest's comfort above all else. She will also consider the fact that they are a married couple and choose option E most of the time. The reason for this answer is quite simple. Having the family visit is a chance for the family to bond.

Putting them up at a hotel at the last minute can be seem a bit insensitive, antisocial, or unprepared, or perhaps not wanting them to stay at the house at all. The lines can be crossed easy, and during sensitive times like these, moments of selflessness are most appreciated and leave a lasting impression.

Sacrificing your own comfort for a guest is not only a noble thing to do, but it is the ultimate level of class.

HOW TO INVITE DINNER GUESTS OVER

If you are planning a dinner party, you must first identify your guest list. Consider the people you are looking to invite. Are these people business associates, friends, or family? Depending upon the nature of your invitees, your invitations can be formal or informal. For business associates and friends, a formal invitation process is most accepted.

For family and close relatives, informal is most accepted. If you have decided that your invitees are in line with a formal invitation process, you then need to decide if you will send out your invitations electronically by email or through the mail.

Text message invitations for informal dinners are a hot button and can be seen as inappropriate, especially for business professionals.

a) When sending your invitations by mail, be sure to include a return envelope with a stamp already affixed.
b) When you are creating your formal invitations, remember to send them at least three weeks from the date, so that you can receive the RSVPs back and organize the

menu based on the diets of your invited guests.
c) Many hosts make meals not considering the dietary needs of those attending. Be sure you have identified the vegetarians amongst your list and prepare your menu accordingly.
d) Your formal invitations should include the date, time, place, dress code, a place for dietary restrictions, and a place to note if they can bring a guest.
e) It is wise to not chose your menu until you have collected all the data from your invitations.

1. SETTING THE DINNER TABLE

Setting the table is extremely important. Knowing what to place where is not only necessary, but it is essential to the ease of the meal. Deciding if you are having a basic casual, or formal dining occasion will help you decide how to set your table as each one is different. This will also help you in understanding what kind of dinnerware, glassware, stemware, and flatware you will need.

Understanding how to set your table is important, but what is more important is knowing what flatware to use when, at what time, and with what foods. Learning all the many pieces and using only what is necessary will save you from the embarrassment or the ignorance of serving salad on a bread plate or serving Bordeaux in a Champagne flute.

This book is merely an introduction and tips that will get you inspired to dive deeper, but you must know there is a difference in a bread-and-butter plate, a salad plate, and a dessert plate. There's also glassware and stemware designed for wine. Both white wine, Bordeaux, and Burgundy have stemware that are best suited for the ultimate tasting experience.

Your overall presentation of the dinner table is just as important as the meal itself. If you are using decorations, be sure that your decorations are not obstructing the view across the table as large decorations can interfere with conversing at the table.

Be sure that they are low enough to allow for an ease of conversing. The decorations should be modest enough to allow the food to be at the center of the table and the primary focal point. The decorations are used to highlight the meal, not to take away from it. Keep the decorations modest and use much of the table space for the food, flatware, and ease of space.

2. BEER/WINES AND ALCOHOL

Serving alcohol at dinner requires a bit of skill and a lot of consideration. If the goal is to have a good time without drunkenness, especially in a formal setting, I would suggest avoiding any dark or hard alcohol as well as limiting beer before dinner. There are a few rules to alcohol at dinner that you should consider.

a) It is not customary to serve beer or dark or hard liquor at formal dinner events.
b) Once you are at the dinner table, only "food complimentary" drinks are served, meaning any other alcohol that the host wants to provide at the event should be served prior to calling all invitees to the dinner table. View the pairing list below to see what drinks work best with such food menu options.

WHITE WINE: Seafood, Chicken, Fish, Pasta, and Salad

RED WINE: Steak, Lamb, Goat, Veal

All About Wines

The look of sophistication and class on a woman who knows her wines—it is timeless.

Some of us are new to the social world of wines and generally have a limited understanding on what makes a good wine, how wines differ, and how to buy them. In this chapter, I will share what I have learned, and hopefully you will learn something new.

Of course, I will first have to share a funny story. About five years ago, I was getting ready for a date as we were heading to a dinner party. He called me to let me know that he was in route and about five minutes from my house. During the short chat, he said, "I forgot to snatch a couple of bottles of wine. We cannot arrive at the dinner empty-handed. Do you by any chance have a good bottle or two hanging around?" In all my ignorance I replied, "For sure."

When he arrived, I grabbed the bottle, rushed out the door, and made it to the car, and there he was smiling, delighted to see me dressed in a simple black wrap dress. He leaned over, kissed my cheek, grabbed the bottle from my hand, and opened the car door. Moments later, the overhead light came on, and he gently said, "Babe, is this the only bottle you have?"

Confused, I replied, "Oh, I have six more bottles of the same one. I can run back inside and grab another." He replied, "No worries. That supermarket across the street, is it any good?"

Moments later, we were in the wine section, hand in hand, looking up and down the aisles, for something I had no clue about. He held my hand tight as he feverishly looked and finally stopped to look at a bottle, read the back, placed it back down, and decided. "We will just bring dessert."

Out of nowhere, an associate from the Beer Din asked, "Can I help you all with anything?" They chatted. He smiled, and he laughed. With full hands, we ended up at the register when the total came up to

$138.04. I was blown away. We only had two bottles of wine, fitting bags for both, and tissue paper. My bottles cost $8.99 per bottle. What was I missing here?

As we made our way back to the car, he said, "Babe, your bottle was fine. It is just not a wine you bring to this kind of dinner party. It is an unbelievably cheap bottle, and these people are wine lovers. It would be an insult. Do not be mad. I will teach you."

While at the party, I realized he got much delight from the compliments of the wine he had brought. To be honest, I really enjoyed the wine I had at home much better, but apparently, the wine we had picked up at the last minute won the hearts of the host and hostess of the party.

For him, that was a win. As a side note, the most expensive bottle of wine sold in history was the 1947 French Cheval-Blanc, which sold for $304,375. To think I was in shock over $138.04 with bags and tissue is hilarious.

HERE ARE SEVEN THINGS I HAVE LEARNED ABOUT WINES.

1. There is an actual market for wine collectors. Yes, people collect rare wines and take it extremely seriously.
2. Never take a cheap bottle of wine to the dinner of a wine enthusiast.
3. If someone asks what region the wine is from on the bottle that you have brought to an event and you do not know, you are in trouble. Get help as soon as possible. These are wine enthusiasts.
4. The top three regions for the most popular wines are Italy, France, and Spain.
5. Every social person/professional should have a wine they prefer. A nondrinker is not included in this, but you should be able to identify your favorite wine and the region its from and describe why you enjoy it. This is a great conversation piece during social events.
6. An expensive bottle does not always equate to a good bottle.
7. There are over 200 different types of wines because there are many varieties of grapes available. It can be overwhelming to decide what kind of wine you like. To narrow it down to about 20, explore and determine if

you prefer a red, white, or rose. This will help you determine what kind of wine you like.

10 MOST COMMON TYPES OF WINE

1. Chardonnay
2. Riesling
3. Pino Grigio
4. Sauvignon Blanc
5. Cabernet Sauvignon
6. Pinot Noir
7. Syrah/Shiraz
8. Zinfandel
9. Malbec
10. Merlot

Wine Attributes

1. CHARDONNAY

Kind of Wine: *White*
Flavor: *Buttery and Oaky*
Country of Origin: *United States*
Food Pairing: *Italian Foods, Pasta, Alfredo Dishes, Duck, Chicken, Hen, Rabbit.*

2. RIESLING

Kind of Wine: *White*
Flavor: Dry *and* Sweet
Country of Origin: *Germany*
Food Pairing: *Great with Pork or Ethnic Foods—African, Asian, Haitian, Jamaican, Indian—Dishes with multiple spices used. Usually dishes with either curry, nuts, or palm oils or multiple vegetables and meats used in one dish.*

3. PINO GRIGIO

Kind of Wine: *White*
Flavor: *Dry tasting, Fruit flavors of pears or apples*
Country of Origin: *Italy*

Food Pairing: Shrimp, Lobster, Scallops, Octopus, Crab, Clam, Oysters, Sea Urchin

4. SAUVIGNON BLANC

Kind of Wine: White
Flavor: Citrus, Vanilla Flavor
Country of Origin: France
Food Pairing: Shrimp, Scallops, Octopus, Crab, Clam, Oysters, Sea Urchin

5. CABERNET SAUVIGNON

Kind of Wine: Red
Flavor: Full-bodied Robust, Heavy
Country of Origin: U.S., California
Food Pairing: Steak, Beef, Bison, Bush meat

6. PINOT NOIR

Kind of Wine: Red
Flavor: Medium-bodied, Cherry and Oak
Country of Origin: France
Food Pairing: Deer, Rabbit, Duck, Elk, Veal, Bush meat

7. SYRAH/SHIRAZ

Kind of Wine: *Red*
Flavor: *Deep Dark, Rich, Pepper Tasting*
Country of Origin: *Australia*
Food Pairing: *Red Meat, Lamb, Goat, Veal*

8. ZINFANDEL

Kind of Wine: *A lighter* **Red Wine**
Flavor: *Earthy, Spicy*
Country of Origin: *U.S., California*
Food Pairing: *Steak or Smoked Meats*

9. MALBEC

Kind of Wine: *Red*
Flavor: Dark, Vanilla, Full-bodied
Country of Origin: *France*
Food Pairing: *Lamb, Duck, Quail, Ostrich*

10. MERLOT

Kind of Wine: *Red*
Flavor: *Spicy, Oaky, Fruity*
Country of Origin: *U.S.*
Food Pairing: *Lamb, Duck, Quail, Ostrich*

Are You Approachable?

No "Resting Bitch Faces"

Are you approachable? This is a question you've may not have honestly answered for yourself or cared to even entertain because somewhere down the line someone taught you to be exactly who you are without ever changing. There is a bit of tragedy in this way of thinking. The tragedy lies in the fact that this way of thinking does not allow personal growth or development. In fact, it ensures arrested development and locks people into one way of being with no true option for expansion.

No one wants to be someone else. That is a good thought, but being your best self is something else. A lot of what we feel is written all over our face and carried in our body language. For many people, they cannot contain their emotions without the truth being exposed in their frown, slanted, or twisted lips, or raised eyebrows.

For others, it simply is an unconscious happening, something that they are not aware of. At some point, these same people have gotten feedback from others saying things like "Well, I didn't feel comfortable coming to you about it" or "You're just not approachable." So, at some point, unapproachable people have heard this before even if they deny being such people.

For those honest folks, being unapproachable is what they like. Some use it as an intimidation factor or to keep people away. Some people find value in what is known as a resting bitch face, or the face of a mad man/woman, but it really is the face of armor.

People who carry the face of armor or the body language of armor believe it is serving them, but what they fail to realize is how they carry themselves teaches the world a great lesson about who they are. If for one moment you thought that being unapproachable was a gift or a sign of strength, I would like you to consider this. Being unapproachable is not a personality trait that cannot be changed or improved upon. It is a learned behavior.

At some point, this learned behavior was further developed, fostered, and added as a way of being. A straight shooter or a "being frank" and straight forward person who has mastered the art of being unapproachable turns into a jerk—that one person no one wants to be around because he is super critical. A "say it like you mean it" woman turns into a bitter and angry person at the first sight of a miscommunication no one wants to disagree with, nor do they want to promote this kind of person.

Being approachable builds relationships, and it allows trust and makes communication easier. People who walk with a sense of openness, warmth, happiness, and excitement about life tend to be better at building teams.

These people are best in leadership roles or in roles where contributing ideas are necessary. These people move up the corporate ladder, quit easily, and are most likely in leadership positions.

If you are looking to improve your chances of walking through doors of success, you must make yourself approachable.

Now keep in mind that approachable does not equate to agreeable, but approachable sends a message to all of those around you that you have no false walls of protection up.

Therefore, you are confident in all your doings.

1. DO NOT SEND THAT EMAIL UNTIL YOU READ THIS

Many times, I have been in situations when I have sent an email wishing I could recall it, especially the ones I have sent when I was fuming or responding to a condescending email sent to me. Corporate America can be a stressful place, especially when dealing with people who are trying to climb the corporate ladder while stepping on your back to get there. These people can be ruthless, calculating, demeaning, and downright unpredictable.

For sure, there is email etiquette that you should always follow, but what do you do when you get an email that puts you on the defensive? What do you do when someone sends you an email as a calculating tactic to protect themselves and throw you under the bus?

You do **NOTHING**. I repeat, do **NOTHING**, well, not initially. Here is why I say do nothing initially. There is nothing more rewarding than taking the high road even in situations where you can clearly see that the person is either taking advantage of a situation or painting a picture of you that is not true. Taking the high road is not only rewarding, but it can save you from moments of embarrassment.

Here is something to keep in mind. Emails at work are supposed to remain professional. No matter the circumstances, they must remain professional. Email is a form of professional business communication, and with that in mind, there is no need for a justification of your feelings. You must always keep this in mind. Give yourself twenty-four hours to respond unless the email was sent from a superior or manager.

If the email was sent from a supervisor or manager, the first thing you must do is walk away from your desk. Take a break, walk, get some air, and have a glass of water. Give yourself a moment to process the information before responding.

If your interest is in keeping a paper trail, give yourself an additional fifteen minutes to process it all. If you respond immediately, you are bound to use the email to be combative, destructive, defensive, or argumentative, all these things are unprofessional and inappropriate.

Instead, give yourself some time, collect your data and all the facts, organize your thoughts, and use the email to present your case.

2. HERE ARE SOME TIPS ON SENDING YOUR EMAIL

a) Always remain polite and professional.
b) Be sure to use the proper opening, greeting, and closing.
c) Be sure you check the tone and use of words.
d) Avoid words like "furthermore" or statements like "as stated in my last email."
e) If the email is a directive, it is more appropriate to ask a question by starting with an action word or phrase.

For example, "Could you kindly provide?" or "I kindly ask," or "It would be helpful if."

a) Try not to overuse intimidating words or words less likely used in the workplace.
b) Be direct and concise but not rude.
c) Keep your email straight and to the point. One paragraph should sum up your email, and anything more than two paragraphs can be lost in translation or otherwise disregarded all together.
d) Try not to CC any unsuspecting person.
e) Do not use exclamation points to drive a point.

I understand that upholding these tips can be difficult, especially if you feel your job or reputation is on the line, but that is even more reason to lead with these. Taking the high road means you will remain a professional even when others are not. You will remain a professional even during times your character is tested. If you can maintain a level head, it points more to your strength than it points to anything else. At this point, you win regardless of the outcome.

3. TIPPING DONE RIGHT

When it comes to tipping, how much do you do? Are you a gracious tipper? Do you measure how much you give based on the services you have received? Tipping is generally what we do for folks in the service industry to show our gratitude.

From the gas station attendant who pumps your gas to the hairdresser, the food delivery guy, or the waiter at a restaurant, these people are working in the service industry, and thus, tipping has evolved into a practice of wage supplementation rather than just a grand gesture of gratitude.

Because tipping has evolved into much of a wage supplementation, many people are faced with the guilt of tipping far too little even if they give the suggested state minimum.

Gratuity has made its way into many areas of our lives. Things have changed so much over the last ten years.

We are finding ourselves in Ubers, Lyfts, and other rideshare options. We are enjoying the convenience of food delivery services, like Uber Eats, Grub Hub, and Door Dash, but most states' minimum wage remains the same. Most of us are aware that tipping is not just a nice thing or the right thing to do. For most service industry folks, they rely on it, so it becomes a must-thing to do.

The question becomes, do you tip everyone the same? Your nail tech and the bartender, do you tip them? Your water delivery guy and your massage therapist, how much do you tip them? Do you tip your eyebrow lady the same as the woman who does your nails? Or do you randomly just give what you feel?

Regardless of how much you tip, I think the socially correct way is to be sure that you are.

HERE IS A LIST OF SUGGESTED TIP PERCENTAGES PER SERVICE PROVIDER;

1. Hair Salon 15%
2. Manicurist/Pedicurist 10%
3. Massage Therapist 20%
4. Eyebrow Services/Waxer/Threading 10%
5. Restaurant Server 15% -20%
6. Bartender $1 per every $5 spent
7. Hotel Housekeeper $3 per night
8. Parking Lot Attendant $1 per stay
9. Full-Service Gas Attendant $2
10. Ride Share 10%
11. Food Delivery 20%

I hope the tips I have shared in this book were helpful. I am still learning each day as I continue this journey through womanhood.

Etiquette to me is just not about social norms or classism nor is it about being accepted.

Class, etiquette, and wealth share the same room, but I have also met some classless wealthy people.

Now that I have said that, you do not need to be rich to be classy, and you for certain do not need money to live your life with class.

Etiquette and class will get you in doors that are otherwise closed to others.

Keep learning and growing.

Much Love,

www.ingramcontent.com/pod-product-compliance
Lightning Source LLC
Chambersburg PA
CBHW042121100526
44587CB00025B/4147